GET LOST

GET LOST

MARTHA ZWEIG

DHP

Oregon

TNPRP
an imprint of DHP
Post Office Box 670, Warrenton, OR 97146

GET LOST Copyright © 2020 Martha Zweig
All rights reserved

No part of this book may be reprinted without the express written permission of the publisher. For permissions, contact DHP, Post Office Box 670, Warrenton, Oregon, 97146.

Printed in the United States of America

ISBN 978-1-935716-40-2

Cover artwork:
World Map Painting on Handmade Paper

Lightman/Shutterstock.com

CONTENTS

Whereabouts	11
Professional Sleep	12
Stone Song	13
Contretemps	14
Pledge	15
She Listens	16
Procedure	17
DOB	18
Custodial	19
Night Owl	20
By Way of Illustration	21
Orange Persona . . .	22
The Bats	23
Abracadabra	24
Spite Face	25
Erotic Complaint	26
Terms	27
Nuptial	28
Sepia	29
What Becomes of Them	30
Rat Song with Undertones	31
Astral & Mundane	33
Calling	34
Stan Frees the Cats	35
Pendulum	36
Railroad Moon	37
Mr. Bluster Housesits	38
Still Hungry	39
March Archaic	40
Wattle & Daub	41
Outfit	42
Foxfire	43
Shingle	44
Fictor's Triolet	45
Landslide	46
White Phosphorus	47
Pomegranate	48
Everglades Field Journal	51
Anhinga Trail	53
Cows	55
Flandrian Transgression	56
Preacherbird	57
Welcome to Senegal	58
Mangrove Bride	59
Alligator Resolve	60
Ding	63
Pachyderm	65
Advice	66
Real Estate	67
Domestic	68
Rebirthday	69
Overturn	70
Portrait	71
Ebb	73
Opthamalogy	74
Exploratory	75
Irrelevance of Angels	76
Towns	77
Pinch me	78
To Distraction	79
At Leisure	80
Cross-Country	81
Intervention	82
Protestant Argumentative	83
Carolina	86
Dogtooth	87
Over Again	88
Provisions	89
After Summer	90
Soiree Vivante	91
What Time It Gets To Be	92
Everybody Waiting	93
Aberration	94
Impulse to Dissolution	95
Accidental	96
Sputter	97
The Worst Over	99
Speculation	100
Let's	101

1   FITS & STARTS

WHEREABOUTS

Glove box rummages itself & dumps: fuzzy cough
droppings & stuck (menthol) among them a misdirectional
map intrigues me: say clotheslines'
fripperies hopping the breeze off the alley & garbage
lids clanging downhill to the sea: say there
in the sea floes
of penguins bobbing up to Argentine flamingos.

How hard is it to get lost? Listen to lost
useless horses whingeing for home & hames, a lost
grail stuffed with dirt deaf to human legends long
unstrung of sacred tune & lost,
children prodded along in the loops of war,
hopscotch mistake, the cast stone
skipped off the lake instead & lost the tournament

to the nice policeman there with the ice cream
precinct & his body buddy Dad. Dad declares he knows
by the spit & stripe of her this's no one of his own,
his kids mope, & he goes. Ear to ear I must
look lucky at last, librarian
at the dictionary of things looking-up ever since
I hid in the glove box, pretending to be directions.

PROFESSIONAL SLEEP

Through the cracks in systematic
application step-by-step, who
has fallen? One by one more than the time
before, with its monotonous hands!
Appointments shift accordingly.

Evening commute

home where the broken bread
butters its inevitable
downside at the left front foot of your chair
where a dog used to press itself who remembered you,
in your absence put-to-sleep professionally.
In your stead resigned. Gist of the matter,
as if to represent itself still open to last-
minute post-suggestion, vacillates.

I, too, make the moment count. I stipulate
to not everything, but a great deal. Trouble I saved
a colleague accrues to my credit: I will be spared.
Lead me from the disheveled field.

When it gets dark, dim even, a song puts me to sleep.
La, a mother may venture, *sink under the satin*
blanket-hem, do your tuck up, let yawn
what shining fissure you've come to tumble into.

Kindergarten teacher entrusted a note home
"Kindness of Martha." Martha deliberately delivers this.
She meant to. She hid it in her agenda. Her dog
ate her; they both insisted the note said to.

STONE SONG

How do we help him, he
cannot get to the end
of the first stone he studies
of its tangled ores

in six colors of veins
it crooks him in
while his tools clash behind:

He said he would scratch, like this,
he taps
he says it has burst into flocks like bats,
he says he is strung on their cries
through the hollow heart he was born with,
it empties, it fills
pushing the rage of the ground
on; he'll sing 'til he dies
black air, the thousands of bony wings.

CONTRETEMPS

About time, you'd think, parental wisdom beyond mere
years kicked in, but shudder thunder
rumble & rain, the dooryard shrub
shamelessly grovels as downstairs their common belated
anniversary slams home, shrugs off the damp in sheer celebrity.
Stricken lightning, ozone simmering.
Which one gets to relax, who gets up to check for utility candles?

*I wouldn't know. I couldn't one
cupboard or drawer from another
reason or rhyme or remember where
it was you or I
put the children for misbehaving the rest
of their lives or how raking it over the whole
neighborhood now is supposed to help*, says he:

& replies she, *I knew it the second its fiery
features sank in that black-cloud scowl that the sun
sets its every disappointment against us,
picks every detail
I worked up from nothing whatsoever to finery:
featherstitchery, loopy frogs, silk-covered seedy
pearls, batting my own iridescent eye lashes!*

Crept to the hall tree hiding, though, us kids expect
belligerent weather still to raise a kind of praise, why not?
--surely deluge delivers its drubbing upon us all & hurls by
on our gratitude off to ulterior hinterlands: *Let's you
& me nibble pixels & fall asleep in the TV
with the evening horrendous news, old pet,
as long as the power lasts.*

PLEDGE

The nation's one
undergod glows in the dark. To its immense
satisfaction cover your heart & allege.

Repeat after me, pistol
packermeister & schoolkid of immemories: *I'm not
gonna stand for it.*
Units of distaste,

privy trough, hogtied public flag about the chinny
chin chins, yum. Ruling classic for all: flog
a misfit for the edification. Prod the glib & glibberty
dissidents up to a dropstep gibbet jig.

Video: Amber waves goodbye &
godspeedy, too. Boo whoo? —you, it's just US of A-

nother disgruntled grunt's shock & aw-shucks
Ameri*Canis-cannibalis*, dog-eat-(hot
diggety)-dog, jackal-of-oil-tirades,
commodieties & the x-change:

hawkitup, yank, & jingo.

SHE LISTENS

Surely you mean me
to understand you. You do not
intend me
to get you
wrong again!—
or every time you say
that, or say anything else.
Surely you talk language.

If you make me
I can show by
exegesis what you
pick your words to
hint me at. Then you
can have me as
crazy as any man
ever put up with!

This is how a man
makes a woman think
all day. So women
think all day.
They think this.
Their quickening fingers weave
strands of the spigot water,
weave water.

PROCEDURE

A man gets in & gets out.
"If you notice any
consequences," he says,
zipping his pants shut,
"we've got a technology."

Men admire a
self-sufficient woman.
"Independent survival,"
they say, slipping the leather tongue
into the buckle, "proves who's human."

"There is nobody her now,"
a woman observes, "but me, my own body."
Also she ventures, "Fetus, parasite!
You use me!" and spreads her
legs as the vacuum machine turns on.

DOB

doom baby doom
oh my dear soul
we hear tell such
fabulous babble, such
tongues

& hunger, fishflesh
bread blood wine, mother's
own tiny tuber

begin benign

CUSTODIAL

Nutshell, nut nugget, last one,
snug one of my children,
sleepyhead in an eggshell, can't you
hear it clap clap daybreak,
clap yellow sunup, clear blue bell?

Anybody's appletree &
any appleblossom's bumblebee
starts up any minute, & then who'll
dare tell three inquisitive hills
just to get on without her?

Hobbyhorse, bear book, baby rose,
paper house & household, whose
do we get to be being hers when she's still
this dreamy so late? Does one-
&-the-same four-legged bed foster us all?

Scare bird, hollow owl in the owl
stories, I know her nights by your big
gold eyes & your splendid wings
she spreads to swoop up the rocking
moon askew in its moonshine,

& if I winked her off to whatever
wanton plots you hatch, I can match the meanwhile:
rapt to hear whatever she'll deign
(or won't) to tell when you drop her home
again, o flaccid claws then, beak lax, unhinged!

NIGHT OWL

Night owl: favorite, it so enjoys its
eyes. Blink! but I was born into such exhausted
light that mother had to cast out
long stories to find me. Chest of her
lunar silver, linens & one mossy pine
chair knocked over murmured they missed me.

Night owl, predator, lifted local cats
out of their lives. I got picked up feral. Mother,
skank puss that she was, plucked peril
out of its hot feathers & fed. Root,
stump, the whole knitted hollow worried & warned
me once & by twice I was long gone.

Night owl, pantocrator, did me its favor.
I'd be its joy. Creatures it killed kissed me.
It loosed mother running into her second wind.
I began to dilate the long vision. Just before ending
up clinched in a low owl's instinct each of the stories
lost track of itself.

BY WAY OF ILLUSTRATION

Work up a sky first: purview a few
watercolors bleed half to death.
Air looks a stench, then ink wets
a trail into the woods. Two runaway children
pluck up animal tracks one after another,
each track tastier than the last, so the two
can't help stuffing themselves all the way to the lair.
There, pigments compound the telling

details until you have disappeared.
But by a worldly demeanor self-
evident around them, the children together
can't yet get lost. The lesser-loved
of the two (by the other) looks like an adventurer:
the sister or brother (or neither) may sulk & dither
until the nicety-brush, three sable hairs, will fix
them both mannerly at a wooden table, their faces

reflecting in bowls of yellow broth, but I can't
any longer distinguish their eyes in the steam. Flavor
of marrow rises & strays towards a glint of weather
the windowpane stops: *No weather allowed in here,
you, you.* Now even the children's names can't call.
Can't call: even if the artist designed
herself the kitchen clock's cuckoo next,
she couldn't summon its twit to change her mind.

ORANGE PERSONA WITH TRIGGER WARNINGS

Halloweening night:
                        steps &
*knock knock who's
there*: This

is Jacko, your own
personal pumpkin eviscerated

Who tells
Who mutters spells
                Who knows
the neighborhood, somebody slipping pest
pellets into the marshmallows for quote-
&-effin-unquote jigaboos
to stifle & die, devils

(soap
their looking glasses fat & skin
their howling lamps)

& somebody donating poisoned
pennies for unicef, so don't you suck even
just one, baby brothers & sisters!—

& this is Jacko too Who
by midnight sputters:
                —O no matter how
I try I can't stop smoking (I'm so smutty black inside)
til I get blown
out by the sweet mother of this house

its rooms
its Novemb'ring beds
as we lie down now with the All
Saints & All Souls sheets

up to our chins mouths closed eyes over our heads

THE BATS

Born snagged in gorgeous guesswork, within
the year I felt my shoulder blades determine to quit
demeaning themselves hankering wings.

Malicious kin put me out to ill fortune.
Take this sack of knots, they hissed, which I hid
amid their sneers, since isn't a knot like a child?

For a spot to sleep, I took up the season's
likelihood of dry leaves with a single high chink
of water, nine or ten salutary minerals.

Something imaginary to eat will do for you,
the cave's inner trickle told me as it no
doubt had the bones scrambled before me.

For divertissement, minims of sentiment,
I made do through an interview among rodents
& rumors & other slight acquaintance

even though I, sworn to the family silence,
and I, appointed the family liar,
and I, of the family vanishingly shy,

replied almost more little than possible.
Never you mind: in the advance of the kindly
dragon they serve, the bats skipped formalities,

bombarded & primped me & curtseyed away
as I'd fly apart recollecting myself
as rumble and rubble as wind as the sulfur dust

shifted clumsy feathers & scales hunkered me down.
I told the dragon my trouble. It sighed;
the dragon rolled its throat & sighed such fire.

ABRACADABRA

The rabbit who lived in the hat took his turn
promenading the woman who lived in the shoe
around & around (winding, wound up)
the alphabet block. Observe: cliques

of Punches, Judies, voodoos & rags adopting
one Zennish riddling expression, a loosely-matching
of pairs of eyes, wrong neighborhoodlums & nobody-
homies our couple

skirted past venturing light salutations, a nod: *Hey
there. Afternoon.*
                        Dear reader, if only your poet's
timelier flourish could've switched us all to birds!
--befitting curtseys & brazenings-out in the street grit--

*They had so many children we didn't
know what to do!* We outgrew, we burst hat & shoe
& stifled the magician at his word. I myself
tweaked off of her chilly witch-tit the last
sniping gutter-serpent's tooth.

SPITE FACE

I duck by with my no
nose in the air. Higher &
mightier now than I, my nose
has cut me off

without a scent, for I
(just like *if thine eye*)
Biblically offend its inspiration.
I suppose it has rarefied.

I, who cannot tell chopping
onion today from any other
fierce tears, say a week's July
dead dragged up & counting,

beg pardon: my features'
mien repugnant the more
than usual, though polite
company hasn't arrived

to say so, insist so, pointing *out
damned Spot*, bad dog, & what a nose
didn't that one have, for the drugs,
news, carrion & the privates.

EROTIC COMPLAINT

I registered my displeasure
under an assumed name. The name came
to mind & dwindled down the corridor after the bags
as I groped my bra top for a tip.

What appeals to authorities? Pass
the alphabet brittle, a shingle, a slab, couple of Mosaic
tablets & sloppy tumbler

of water, my effing head
gee aches. Hi, j(ac)k; element-of-pique, our
estuary— hence the tumultuous settlement-down
like migratory fowl in a flurry of all-around congratulations.

Dearest, offend with me
the best, the yet; next-enumerable commandment
just distinct through the twintowering babble
all concerned endure over which hospitality
policy best adjusts the standard
risks of lust. A silver
service hustles into suite 2-B, where my reiterant
animadversions (concerning hyenas, say; petticoats,
upright piano, military adventure, mayonnaise, Hector the pup)
& I slosh
the sheets in gooey golden-goose-
egg tempera washed up with moonshine—

careless, tonight, to proceed
upon otherworldly goings-on
& farther-flinging, even, than these?

TERMS

But I moved on, I shoveled my
slick soul out from under its
brown habit & sludge, so yes I'll
love you— I'll start right now! It's
four already; we'll be done by
six Tuesday, outside.

Honor bright my word's as good as
yours is by the common kindness
—he said & she said—
I don't mind you lick my nice
body some, but just you don't
sniff my kitchen to break bread.

NUPTIAL

Cold hearts & crafty of the
maple & the mild ivy have laced
her ready in her green shapely
dress to marry; she may
court no other than the one other they'll wind,

who, in time
mercifully goes himself so
leafy she need
know no face of his own,
nothing unbearable; & though the
firstborn plies at her flimsy & sallow, it's
welcome sworn hazel, hello
there little willow.

SEPIA

The snow sags & the
kids' sleds' runners
sink through into mud. Nobody
wants to visit the dirty hill
now. *What
else is there to
do?* Everything there was before

to do is still here.
The kids come in & stand there.
Mitten strings hang out of six sleeves.
Soft ice clogs four
boot clasps. All three
have wet knees,
mother

has a hill,
has a sled there was before, & what
else there was to do, & has mother too who
drained down into the ground &
father who drained into the ground too;
hard times sometimes, mother there we were,
we stood on the newspapers dripping.

WHAT BECOMES OF THEM

Cluttered with extra sleeves &
scarf-ends flapping, she'll go
brace herself in the loud ledges.
Soon sky blows gold here & fish
switch under the foamy sieves.
From choppy light & appetite, birds spot
morsels they'll drop & slosh for &
lift away.
     Think of the brilliant &
shifty children! Now they hold the ends of the earth
& flip fancy nets upon the godforsaken. Hear
them still bawl their unmistakable notes!

—while the ocean itself, in high breast &
all piss-&-vinegar, souses & oompahs at the
cliffs, drubbing kelp mats &
mussel beds. Punchy clouds double
over windward.
       Ever since earliest
nursing she knows that astringent
pang deep in the uterus;
it puckers after the three otters below
borne up on three swells.
They loll until they tuck to immerse themselves,
slick as a whistle.

RAT SONG WITH UNDERTONES

Hop the sill
of my sleep, old rat. Whose hold
scrambled you out?
Stutter against me, thirsty & thin,
scratch to come in, and I let the rat

enter my nostril, let the rat sniff
the teeth in my jawbone one by one;
tug at my vocals, whose else's
voice but mine could the voice be? What else
could it do but speak for me?

Downstairs guests mutter in the window dressing.

***

Rat hanging around, edge of my seasick
supper, another hunger we share,
mess-kitchen inquisitor I never
saw before but as other, survivor & heir,

we must've plucked up together awash in high verbiage:
slopped up in the ocean, the brown foam rats cross,
shipboard & sinking, in harbor in squalor,
in throats of the poor, their infants & elders,

in bed with stones, in the oven with stones,
apart at the fork & steaming milk,
rats in their juices, a meal.

Downstairs the filaments safe in their bulbs go off, on.

***

What crosses a rat's mind uppermost?
No idea, this is one of the rats
of the no-idea at all:

skitterings, brain-stammers, frigidity,
sneers & whiskers, sharp snout
probing the stale poison, twitching the walls

of the paper song, convulsing my hem in a scurry:
the broom comes, the cruel & bristly
broom from the other room, from the pantry & tub

where the potatoes rub & the baby
buried there lest the authorities.

Downstairs a clever Christmas tree assembles a bicycle.

***

Who did I wind up a tin
rat to be? My buddy, my jolly,
my cuddled heart,
mothers' anathema, shock my mother & flee,

hit the crawl spaces, spatter the dock, I shove off
with the rat in a lunchbox, brave as a sandwich,
running for life, for the new land,

founding a species, a spangle of moon-hangings,
wrestle & rock in the bag in the burlap & drum,

the rat singing its chatter its chuckle,
my choice, my carriage & passenger.

Downstairs the piano
sheets another piece of its yellow music.

ASTRAL & MUNDANE

Is it worse to be or to be friends
with the poor girl of the brown dowry?
Her father limps away from the door & leaves
her as if she might play.

This nocturne won't ever
slip out to play again: she broke its key
in the slot. There goes the other father waving
his own hand vaguely behind himself hurrying off.

Hocus-pocus swoops the neighborhood's one
huddle of shrubs, wand shedding a gust of glitter half
sharps-&-flats & half statistics. Bedtime's network tugs
the other children up into warm loose knots.

Whoever gets singled out must die. She stayed
in the thicket with small animals renowned
for their namelessness. Who can invite
anyone over, then? Who can even call anyone home?

CALLING

Here come the lost:

some in clods, others maybe in calico madcap & finery,
edging along their long lost ways.
Where have you been?

Morning and night as I opened up and shut
and embellished the lids of my eyes you disappeared
without having appeared again,
and never appeared again.

Where were you?

To my parents, I was lost. My mother
called, my frantic father
called, silly & sad, while I sat right there
in my blistering personal filth,
in my flaming hobgoblin gown with the lunatic
fringe & the patriots' blood-dragged hem. *Please
pass the butter* I said,
but they leaned farther out into the dark & called.

Where are you?

Long-gone animal familiars! Gone feral or killed or stricken— I can't tell
any one of them's bitterest end from its
own or another one's wholly other
& luckier life because they are lost to me.

STAN FREES THE CATS

The padlock undoes to his hands
given like the egg of keys.
In the pound's middle moonlight he

gestures them, captives, go on, and they do
at once, all trotting straight along the
steel fence shadow, their tails floating,

and out the gate, where they lengthen & bound:
*Avengers' joy to them now, survivors! So-called
mercy indeed to mercykillers!* They'll prowl

no dwelling Stan rests in, pry no curtains there, sip
no breath out of the babies— even as Stan too
readjusts discipline. He dismisses

cats, he drills Red revolution.
We inch towards the actual curb.
We size up the next block.

PENDULUM

Error creeps in, eats up the children's alphabet: song,
soup & cipher, error soon seen
to make itself comfortable, thrive. Likewise have untold other
barbarians done, locals today & homely, just trying to live.
Error admits itself among strange-to-itself legitimate
citizens whether otherwise or by somewise else.

I'm telling you why: because I say so! barks even the dead
silence left of our patriarch, he who saw
our bloodline's descent snarl into depravity.
I ooze vicissitude into my own sheets. Who will tuck
me in among such mummies as priests once drained to bind
in long sticky strips into that tranquil posture?

Really— I used to romp about in such generous love!
I was just darling. Let's not get sick over this. I cracked
books & picked along pages mumbling as error
wandered them overleaf, subtext & underside,
window birds jittering nervously *hint*
or *hint* until, unbeknownst, my love

burnt out on its rickety rocket to hang the moon
from a yellow gallows & there it glows,
confessed & sentenced innocent— do come see!
Other motley youngsters career about as the moon
in moon doom swings from error
to error above the rising rosy ash of an evening's breeze.

RAILROAD MOON

You've noticed the moon's bruises.
Must've. She's a good risk. She'll still
show up right on time in her black-&-blue;

so hire the moon and count on her to
air your sheets of cocky
profit-&-loss and straighten out your ghost books.

On the side she'll soon be turning
tricks for you with the souls of trains like
dreams when they shunt in or out

on down behind your bleak &
backtrack room. Pay her in poems. She eats
human poems out in the slow yard nights.

MR. BLUSTER HOUSESITS

Trot the dog along the whistling graveyard.
Humor the dog of the lady who's Not Home,
but whose neighborhood's also Not Famine & Not War
all day long.

All roads range & return. The dog
fetches in such delight the keys you tossed you toss
the keys again, & then in your unguarded
instant stooped at the lady's door the dog
sticks a sloppy tongue in your ear.

Drunk disease has that lived-in look, shape of the couch.
The TV fumbles among remotes, finds whatever it wants
until you want whatever it finds: species reportedly
local to the body hair in hovels, tracks of international

infant tears, but keep
your cheeks to yourself & hands to thy service,
o distant Lord whose overseers
visit to overlook.

The dog kibbles, the dog resettles a round bed that it likes.
Not the dog's soul, then, scratching: nip in the air,
whines to get out, catching a fleet scent of itself on the ill

wind blowing the no-good
up & away & head-over-heels with the pro-
&-con man. Huff puff, the con man breathes.
The house staggers up & down.

STILL HUNGRY

October: steepening porch steps: night
stumbles over the last light & falls.
Interior: wolf spiders nudge up the drains
to spread themselves in the bathtub
or nestle the wet cups in the kitchen
sink while you
who are no fun at all
clear up after our meal.

How can we fold
into our homemade bedding upstairs,
your side, my side?
—to commend to each other's use what heat
informs our bloods? —each
overhearing the other's heartbeaten
blood run from beginning to end
the nightmare canyons of the ruined room?

Let's shrug off every & all
zazen protocol tonight. Let's both our breaths
stagger around wild, catch up at slight & slack
like the single silks the other
spiders in other
seasons cast to attach. You'd think
what little love yet
remains to us could do us what little good.

MARCH ARCHAIC

Here chances penniless
Death along the bunny trail,
mouth snapping up old snow. He'll swap
one of his chewy-knuckles for love.
Yum, says he.

Strop me a bit of green steel for his hunt!
—but he will take nothing but love.
No twisted hide thong, no twig
cage brimming with yellow eye-light.
Yowl, says he.

Spin him a lovers' story: enmesh
his wit in its idling curiosities, quick
switches & knotty identities; keep Death guessing
the riddle that takes nothing but no for its answer! but O
yes, says he.

Send for my father, dragging his ring of kingdom keys.
Turn over my mother to primp & sing,
but Death scoffs. Then let me deliver to Death, dear, our own
newborn, laughing & paddling her pink arms! but no:
Only you, says he.

WATTLE & DAUB

Anna put the fire to rest
in its kitchen slot. Then under
the window loosened a mouse
latch a little, or some other such
hinge itching with rust
against a molding.

Dark out: fields of bat stitches,
the cabbage & potato patches,
a pocket crust or crumb just
about to get plucked up. *I lost
my love, oh, oh*. Rags adjusted the body
to size. Whose shoes best fit.

For some time owls grooming
the premises kept in touch.
Dust sat minding things.
One adventure after another Anna
yet missed most her spider,
having admired it: *Oh, web!*

OUTFIT

Chilly creek water scoots the last of the stripped
trees' rags through rocks. Underneath dark ice
minutely snowspeckled overnight, the odd
bubble of trapped air wriggles this
way & that, all but organism—

Say I absconded with my little life!
All October this woods blew to tatters &
fussed over its clutter in skittish leaves;
now it preens itself taller & sleek
in its most elegant dishabille,

& so as I mull over for my peculiar
humor what we will wear today, I'll pick
among frayed browns, siennas to umbers, & slick
black like these not-quite-heart-
shaped toothy damp popple flags.

FOXFIRE

Gone this morning, a person I put to bed
all last night long & loved, has left me the fingers
& wrists I wriggle into, my size,
& the warm feet I put on: new woman.

Mirror eye I glance off of Mother
Nurture's eye the can-fool, look at me skip
the hanging closet, the empty
necks that ill-became me, the banishing sleeves!

Will you eggs & crusts
for your breakfast, Your Likeness? I will, & bestow
for the service this pink taint, little lip blot, & for mama bird
at the lilac a hairy comb to pluck.

Will you remember us? Will you forgive us
& carry away our wish? Poor wish —to please! Suggest
our guess, & hustle our schemes to what success & rest they find?
But I am already preoccupied in leaving her behind!

SHINGLE

Mother spoke skua:
she shrieked. Who can roll back
the Atlantic scandal?

I turned my mother's back, punishment enough.
I tutored myself in sand-
castling & scullery, balanced the tide trade;
over the years'
rubble netted & hauled handsome profit.
In exactly the time
it takes to, I can unzip a fish.

Now I've selected a claw,
fastened hanks of snarling hair & ear from shell
to shell, pinned
a chitin chip clustered among dark ochre bladders,
the sea weed.

The ocean rises to greet me, rest of its little
children in tow from jetty out to the moon row.
We'll all wear foam, film, & the long salt sash
in single file.

Safekeeping: is this
where we leave
behind our shoes?
Are you sure?

Thunderation! —the white dog
barely tips its tail, then
whelm, whelm.

FICTOR'S TRIOLET

My fictitious characters make me nervous.
Once I make them up, though, they might change my mind.
If Duke outwits Trix to find Ace...? But because

my fictitious characters make me nervous
I try to keep myself inconspicuous,
seep into the shrubberies I plot behind
fictitious characters. Still makes me nervous,
though. They might make *me* up, once they change my mind.

LANDSLIDE

Ticker shift: clockworkaholic heart
expels what blood it admitted & roundabout
the blood slushes sufficient to oxygenate
my morning dream, ratcheting up
its plot's incidents twice, thrice
too ingenious now to go on: alarm.

Eyeopener: yestermorning's tentative
stress crack still creeping the windowpane.
Bird? A gust? Torque upon temblor
subterra? Ere my foundation slumps
on its underpinnings like dowager aunt's
formerly philanthropic endowments,

I will up & scurry my citizenship out of house &
home on this tectonic errand: 25-zillion-dollar-
a-plate political ticket pluck't from the rubblesome
world rolling-over its bling-bling. Take my quadrennial
best shot, the one we know can eke out
somebody's eye, put out somebody's living.

WHITE PHOSPHORUS

Gaza, 2008-2009

Today I shot all the fish in the barrel
dead then strafed an entire
cemetery targeting each unearthed
body bit bigger than ten
centimeters zeroing in on my cold-
seeking drone.

Little bullets shuttled the mineral
rubble back & forth in slime.
I am exquisite
in timing, I'm history's texts attuned
by lute to the blood thrumming
my ear, the ear alive.

I am King Shit
the sublime. I hear the homing
hum brimming from all Zion's fine
motor coordination in orchestra;
in goggles' green night
vision diaspora rides aurora.

POMEGRANATE

For grief I like something picky.
Here, for yours, I recommend this most
labor-intensive fruit. It will certainly
take you the whole rest of the howling
afternoon to eat.

Busier than the bee,
busier than the nastiness in insides,
the unmentionable— you'll find you'll peel,
pluck & nibble away & not
once look up for any of your loves, I

promise: probe the obstinately coherent
pomegranate with fingers devolving back
to their intimate ape-nerves, infinitely
you'd rather than chip some tool,
it's better than lice, even.

Never do you get less in any
sweet sip life has to offer of any
juice more implacably occupied
by any bigger, bitterer seed.
It is that good.

2 A STRANGE PLACE

EVERGLADES FIELD JOURNAL

ghazal with Sapphics, for Agha Shahid Ali

Paradise: Adam fancied every beast & bird by name.
Likewise his plants & minerals, each administered by name.

Alligator, little green heron, bittern,
gumbo limbo, cormorant, coot, anhinga;
great blue heron, roseate spoonbill, mangrove,
kingfisher, willet.

Fluent among otherworldly aliens' slick evasions,
language insinuates human habit word by word by name.

Strangler fig, bromeliad, sawgrass prairie,
vulture, purple gallinule, saw palmetto;
laughing gull, solution hole, saltwort, glasswort,
pelican, osprey.

Doublechecking my short list of unspecified phenomena
I found I'd disqualified first, second, and third by name.

Cooter, wood stork, liguus snail, bald eagle,
white-crowned pigeon, pond apple, snowy egret;
glossy ibis, horrible thistle, cattail,
red-bellied turtle.

Tepid topics bruit about scientific colloquia.
Eavesdrop: six extinct hypotheses, four overheard by name.

Soft-shell turtle, red-shouldered hawk, great egret,
boat-tailed grackle, Halloween pennant, cypress;
resurrection fern, no flamingo, sulphur,
tricolored heron.

First take an interest, then take more intimate liberties:
beck & call— pet, wife, slave, the native nations conquered by name.

Periphyton, julia, marl, night heron,

duck potato, arrow-shaped micrathena;
zebra longwing, spatterdock, slough, red milkweed,
bladderwort, whitetail.

A ghost entered my vocabulary. All day long it played
fast & loose with the dubious distinctions conferred by name.

Hammock, air plant, diamondback rattler, bay head,
duckweed, slash pine, crocodile rumor, fire ants;
limestone, Nike missile site, canis minor,
swamp lily, viceroy.

Awkward moment! I had to introduce ten friends & neighbors
among ten household appliances, manufactured by name.

Spanish moss, phragmites, exotic birder,
live oak, ram's head, apple snail, morning glory;
horseshoe crab, dawn shutterbug, spider lily,
chigger, mosquito.

Insufficient to know. How do you know you know what you know?
(Mind the self-evidence philosophers discovered by name.)

Panther rumor, borrow hole, crow, white ibis,
garfish, moor hen, gator hole, palm, mimosa;
cedar waxwing, Florida whites, anole.
Marsh rabbit? —Limpkin?

Each creature insists on its own individuality!
How did who get mistaken for me? Martha wondered. By name?

ANHINGA TRAIL, WITH SEMINOLE WARS

Invasive exotic, top predator,
irresistible entrepreneur,
we make short work! —detonate
nations & nuke lunch, pluck
the motherly millinery egret;
dig, scrape, pave, sell,
nutrify, flush, minutely manage,
extravagantly charge. What credible wild

beast or bird wouldn't this very morning shriek
& leap to rip out our gore?
What in the world

is this? —yet another wink-wink-
nudge renegotiable treaty,
artificial pretty pond & its obliging creatures?

—as if white furious
masters & furious hand-over-
fist investors, & furious black
slavery malcontents & furious
so-called "Indian" dispossessed,

tracking each other
furiously for the rest of their lives,

all lost their minds

at once & circled,
straggled haphazard
into an intermission no one foresees,
stumbled upon each other slogging slough

& just stood there

mildly all day,
blinking, curious, kindly disposed,

having forgotten what in the world

their business is, having mislaid their nature?

COWS

*Who in the world do you think
you are, to protect ME?* I guessed
I heard an underlying alligator hiss,
but it was just my losing mind
nosing up from the something-
fishy-always-going-on subconscious.

As for the alligator, a cow!— she
(we think) has no idea. All her life
she has not one, & slides a muddy tuft
to doze, cold-blooded, soaking up rays.
"Hasn't moved" (a man remarks)
"since we stopped here 3 years ago."

As for the cow, Holstein back home
in Vermont, mapped black-&-white
like the world crowding America, she
has no idea either. *They took the calf.
They take the milk the milk the milk the milk.
I met a fish once, in the pond, a small one.*

FLANDRIAN TRANSGRESSION

Acreage: a tract.
I've given the matter
considerable thought. Asleep much
of the time I give the matter I seem
in charge of momentarily over to slack
detritus & seep,

neglect, immemorable;
vegetative acid percolations,
fishy & larval slough. A cognition
laps them as my distant north & south
glacial ices sweat & collapse. Awash, awaken,
arise on all sides

of the proposition at once. What next?
Shiny marl shingle inland,
almost inches of new
brink. The smaller the shapelier
property: its constricting
frontage itches, *I can hardly wait.*

PREACHERBIRD

Hunchbacked, somewhat:
—pulpit posture. A long-nosed
nearsighted elder squinting the righteous
text, spelling it out: *Dread,*
dread the debauched spirit!

Ironhead, North America's stork,
formerly bringer of human babies each in its own
snug spotless sling,
happier luck than a broken arm
to the good people:

when will it prod
the executive movers-&-shakers
together in strict ranks of strict
wooden rows

& make them kneel,
grant them a moment to bow down
their heads to pray,

—enough! —
& then bore them to death,
slowly, o
with its sermon?

WELCOME TO SENEGAL

Monster yam, Florida air potato,
hoists the green tent of itself hoisting itself
over everything of a non-potato
kind, cuddling Florida under itself

like the motherly vegetable circus
you ran off to join as your flaming yam-
dangling act caught on. Every circus
surges to take in a newfangling yam.

Who's invasive? Air potato, native
of Senegal, experts say, shipped over
in slave cargo. Rebel slaves joined native
rebels & fought til it never is over,

but Florida itself was Senegal
in Pangaea: welcome to Senegal.

MANGROVE BRIDE

I admit I was adopted. "Abducted, -ducted, -ducted," clatters the spoonbill, envious from the first. Pneumatophores poked up in that neighborhood, the crib that breathed, soon my fort. Common babies bobbed around the bend like so many vegetable Moseses, until heartless happenstance might tuck them in, no one objected. But I was chosen!

Remember what of my planet? (You ask.) It got overtaken. Currency went electronic & you had to affect a natural-born glitch. Kindred spirits hunkered as best we could in a safe house with a combination. Zero hour when the mangroves landed my sibling prodded me out into a virtual fold of their picnic, where, satisfying themselves as to no more consequential infestation, two of their curious coaxed me aboard. Rising off, the first, most, & last I saw of my planet was a harmless fiction suspended in disbelief.

My wedding day I slipped on marl. I smeared myself, minimal disgrace. I recognized my consort, unambiguously the one: in tepid shallows he stood far out in his own right, a real individual. His looks! —a flush private corporation, interlocking spiders' initial public offering. I grabbed on & hoisted this way & that up into his body, where, as by mistake, I let drop my apartment key. It slid into the snarl & perplex of his enterprise, hopelessly lost.

What adequate mounds of storm debris he compiles for me! All my days I meditate & mortify supine upon my bed of his pneumatophores. Slight torment tickles my bones. Attentive: his thick leaves over me systematically expurgate from circulation salt & yet more salt, the little crystals glitter along his underlips.

Attaining enlightenment, I will become an exchangeable gas.

ALLIGATOR RESOLVE

Where something ought to be
but nothing is and nothing
else is,
I'll squirm,

scour & scrounge up a berm
& begin to rescind
long-delegated authorities,
disembellish the odd

holiday tree I must've put up
in the human mind, if the glacial
impulses any longer remember.

Big ice mount the low water,
little ice wallow high
& succumb, salt sweet
& savory,

upon the famous dust
feed, feed, feed, fattening chance.

3 ODDS & ENDS

DING

January: elementary
playground: athletic field: the park: chain links
in icicles ring the rink. Snowflakes rollick around.

*

Someone turns sotto voce: hung
with tiny gilt lily-
of-the-valley bells, mother's pink ears ring.

*

The rosy ring was plague,
the children skipping & singing
did all fall,
it was awful.

*

Overwrought from overwork,
each hand wreaks
havoc wringing its other.

*

Don't use that ladder!
Get rid of it right now!
One after
another all those terribly-
wrong rungs.

*

Rough trunks-to-tails, elephants circled
the spotlit ring. Or weren't they bloody
satin trunks? — two
boxers clinging & staggering.

*

Bring bring
me the other telephone!

*

Express register: cash in, cash
out, ring year
out year in:
time slots, vital statistics, incubators & morgue drawers,
orderly compartments of change.

PACHYDERM

I packed my grandmother's trunk & in it I
put the alarming blaze out with the cat
whose 9 tales told
such wildly divergent versions.
                                              Under prolonged
interrogation was usually where my grandmother
knelt & deferred:
an ankus, somebody's
proud scarlet howdah.

Trumpet stuffed in her luggage, grandmother never forgot
a single path: fork past the acacia, baobab,
camphor, deodar; then, as elm I seldom

mistook her for, she always
added a ring a year. Among her eldritch
fingers little flames purred.

ADVICE

I talk to the cats
because they are beings.

So are the appliances, but, o,
the cats!— apter they

to see through me—
I may take my liberties & shove

off to Buffalo, say, where in winter the snow-
plows digress to evict

long blocks of freshfallen souls until the streets chime.
I may shine.

Or my foreign correspondent
may mail me a seed:

*Plant in a shallow dilemma during Woebetide,
inches apart.* Nextdoor

lady my age adopted part of the missionary
position over a wheelbarrow

& says she lived. She swears by blue funk: mine
works wonders for her hectic flush

even as her cats affect stupor— six lives one-
to-nine near comatose & none-

the-wiser, I bet they hope I think:
mind my own cryptic instinct.

REAL ESTATE

I hold my peace at 472 Road Closed,
first place uphill of the iffy municipal flood-
deflection project, expected to last
years. O helicopter I

spot daily overhead, whose rotors gently homogenize
an air quality, intercede for me.
Such impulses of mine ascend, I am ashamed to say.

Heir-&-assign of the neighboring deed, whose hut
encumbers & humiliates both properties,
joins me for festive dessert. He contributes his whipped
topping, dribbles the silver jimmies. A mixed
blessing is how he phrases it as the board
groans, & soon away

he goes. Flip then the doormat, grit to grit. Come bedtime
I'll settle in with a relic of broken soap in my mouth
& perish the thought. Wit's end: uttermost
twitch of a fiberoptic,

yet satellites still
bounce mere TV among the fluttering saucers. Disconnecting
a crockpot I seem to get warned
repeatedly to seize my tongue.

Decade it was ago, three
of my scruffiest acres schemed to secede, but I
caught on in time.

Ad infinitum! —plots & spies.

DOMESTIC

Where innocence is concerned,
I keep a culprit: boon companion, house pet.
Also I have my doubts.

Or others took first pick, stuck me
with the lively conscience. Yap yap, or I hear it chewing
velvety slippers under my mind.

Knock: I adopt an adult bearing to answer the door.
A tract? A summons? Oil pipeline hookup day
pumping away my share? But a mere

evening stumbles indoors out of the blue.
Or, nine by now malingered into five, the Daily Grind
flops to my stoop, whose cutting-edge

undoings cancel each other out: void leads,
void ads & items: local oblivion's scrapbook-of-
record sentenced in cumulative absentia;

or the voluminously obsolete
encyclopedia salesgirl, here arrived to settle in per her walking
papers' overfamiliar address?

She will tell me, make myself at home.
She says, *Give it a rest. Give it a moment's*
thanks. Let's eat what you've put behind you.

REBIRTHDAY

Lucky day lottery: I post
my entry wherever law prohibits the void.
Say I submit my 25
good deeds or less, each to its brown parcel
pending reappraisal. What more
(I contend) could a normal person need?

Heroics: I started the day breathing, mouth-to-mouth.
Welcome back to the calendar! Recovery
assigns its rooms first-come,
occupants subject to random
locker-check & confiscation of items. Install, please, a few
fewer urgent engagements & in a more orderly manner.

Wet gray lunch tray: today I favor the house loaf &
mushroom gravy. I used to like appetite best illicit
in a vinyl booth, next to the local wordsmith with a little
smoky alcohol; I liked the burning-cold
sopping cotton swab he helped me to,
then puncture & plunger, ah,

but, as I was just about-to-be saying,
the mind I meant to speak tonight taught heart-to-heart
an antic you need to know. Just try: your second wind
won't snuffle any of those candles out.
Every wicked fizzle reignites. Next-
to-last gasp you won't even wish.

OVERTURN

for Philip

Hi, power, who a hippo were, rough & river-
rocky horse & now (early spring & swollen) cow-
brown, with a will's way over me upside-down.

I queried a willow: wisp, what will a power allow
me of my clamor, whistle of a chilly little
bird misundervoiced so pitifully? Poor bird,

advice, advicious. Power's will not mine that I'd
in any likelihood enlist. Down-headed twit, in all humility,
power too blameless to bother a flick-feather about.

Hello, lower power, plow-prowler, what will you
want of me now that that I've ill-gotten again?
Flower-follower, under the plucky petals of love

before & after the love-not, worm I admire,
mouthy gut, processor, earth-passager? *O just admit*
me once to your dearest & most confidential ear.

PORTRAIT

In the park each spring each nondescript
tree starts up in its flowers the fruit
the Bible says you'll know it by.

Raindrops splat the petals back
like the sour gloves milady took
to her wet spots; wept, wept

in public on the first bench that wrought
itself in vines and scrolls. She sat
on the damp slats against black tendrils.

On blinding summer days, the common
popularities of shade include
a moment's blotto in the woman's brain,

cool eyelid kisses as the leaves
stoop between her face and the infernal
radiance: the sun bangs a tambourine,

hops blue banners in quirky air
that roisters up enough dust to manifest
the dead, soon to subside on her red shoes.

Each leaf tells her a plain green lie.
She thinks that the lies people owe her,
long overdue, will gather like this,

into one elegant green head that admits
feathered friends on quick innocent
errands (or less) that nobody minds,

but the two or three scurrilous
children up there will have to come down
right now, dinner gets so cold.

Autumn nuts, acorns, the horsechestnuts

aglow within split husks— by then she will again expect
abundance at minimum.

EBB

In my good night's
sleep high tide
of my dearest rancor turns.

Nary a moon
shied me any glint of it.
Then this little shift, a

fish switched its
dorsal ripple opposite &
slack took over. Black water,

blood flavor, settles off
shouldering stone. Reliefs
of ribbed sand rise.

Out to sea slides
flood temperament; it tows
some wrack along as some

lapses to drain behind:
dainty placations kinked in matted
sargassum, mineral chimes.

OPHTHALMOLOGY

Pox & scars: nightfall & the moon
seeps out to take a turn
for the better or worse. Stars contagious; dark:
insects & bats catching. Spots
slide in among the wash waters. *We two
rolled like dice & came up such snake eyes.*

Picked alive between the numbers one
to infinity, I'd've liked never better
than tucked to bed, loved a minute, then cried so foul.
Heart's bottom you drew
my happiness from & slipped into it lies
like a trout lake sickening, limp brown by dawn.

Stale breaths inquire door
to door in town. Daylights hang the windows.
A paper bag skids: three sparrows investigate.
So the local crises of consortium pass,
and over the years my eyes' vitreous
humor dries little by little, casting a few black floaters.

EXPLORATORY

When the moth smacks the windshield
the man at the wheel wakes up, still
in a dream of his son's blood
spread between slide and coverslip
and the pinstriped technician's
tiny white hands
hushing the round mouths of vials.

As if he heard a dignitary snip
a ribbon to open the highway,
birds rise off the meadows on either side
to flock to his darkness,
to beat his sleep with their wings
like the air
he flutters in as the two loose ends.

No one can say a word to them,
incredible green surgeons with no hair.
They introduce instruments
where we never are.
You will not dare, he cries.
Let me be light enough. Let the
highstepping powdery moth alight.

IRRELEVANCE OF ANGELS

A radio preacher, having proved that angels
exist, declares that they are also relevant.

Yet surely a god
knowing everything knows
the crush of significance, & sometimes
in the great grace of being beyond
contradiction blinks for the span of a sparrow:

knows that where laundry
lines on pulleys thread upper stories
of tenements, some errant
milkweed puff hopping the windowsills
may light on a clothespin, all
insensible of that innocence which has
no intent whatever, quite without
referent, not necessarily seen.

TOWNS

You arrive and the towns
come to life. The hardware
stores open at last, they display
weathervanes, knives. Already
the sidewalks are chalked for
hopscotch; the first
child drops a stone into the easy first square.

Start over. The towns
come to life. You just stop for
something to eat. The two
coins by the saucer, the last tip, aren't
there for you. But they mark
the table you take.
Then the waitress takes the two coins.

You come to life.
Never thought of it before. Mistake
most people don't make?
Start over. See if it happens again
in any or how many other
towns like this you sooner
or later probably get to.

PINCH ME

During the bank holdup the potted palm
sifts light among sparkling motes of dust
riding the air-

conditioned air from between the blind slats.
Personnel & customers hold perfectly still. Last
night's floor polish

varies reflections in swirls depending
where you stand. A parcel: the cash: slight
gun muzzle gesture:

the thieves bow out. Sighs, then alarums, yells.
I don't want my money anymore,
at least not right now.

On my way home who should I
bump into but you again, bright blue June day
crosswalk spirit.

Nothing from nothing cometh:
a comet, compulsive poet whose tail
leads the body.

TO DISTRACTION

For instance, if I fancy fancy
bedclothes with a sex stain in the satin,
an ancient Christian
saint in Latin with lions
munching his loins & the chic civic
ladies in bleachers flapping the flies, flies
& sighing *ooh ah* will intrude.

Crick of sunshine cripples a cornice
into my mossy alley & here lurches that tipsy &
lingo-overladen clown-taxi again,
straight into the "Permit Only!" I posted affront
of my sweaty setup wordshop:
applecarts' upsets & multiplicities'
upshots altogether ungainly sprawl

upon, say, last week's snub (I'd assumed
subsumed by now) rousing in vivid yellow
bruises to spout my verse. Overhead how many
lightbulbs does it take to change
which one into what next? Puff of what dust
I kick into what ashes I will, won't mine own eye
wink & wrinkle a grin, taking a shine to me?

AT LEISURE

Somebody's poem after a moment's nap, & nap
after somebody's poem is how this afternoon
soaks behind my eyes— as the petals
flutter to pebbles in intermittent sun-wind-
& shade-showers one early May when the backyard
path that never went far took the long way
around to the edge of enough flowering-plum
cumulus to lavish upon any one life,
at once shaken, scattered high, & intact.

What time?— here's only me, whom I utterly
trust to be, & not once yet disappointed;
whose innumerable miscellanies
simply perpetuate the many through
the many more: rise, sink, hover & crisscross
concurrently as schools of coral-reef
fishes do, flash & commingle in a single three-
dimensional transparency rarely
disturbed & never disrupted. Even

sexual love (poor thing, which decrees whatever is not
forbidden compulsory) in such
traces as may cling (especially in my hair
I love to smell, to wind one arm in my hair & tug
across my face to seize it in my teeth) easily
flickers into that happiest-birthday collie pup
who'd grab fast into a brown towel & growl
deep behind her jaws while I hauled her resisting,
mightily as she could, forward into this idyll.

CROSS-COUNTRY

Skis underfoot, I was playing at remuda—
just in my ears, at first, because, stride
for stride, the leathery snow
creaked up at me like saddle-on-horseback:
thought next I'd neigh. Call this
landscape, for instance, Montana, sunstruck plateau wideopen

& all around it the wintry scrub
roan-colored hills neighborly shoved
their ridges into each other, stiff
gray deciduous manes abristle.
Here & there deep dog
flounces broke up the trailbank;
must be ole
Bluff, run on
ahead from the start, flushed hares.

Never thought dinnertime; let loose
ends of mind flap around. Then when the turnoff

dropped into deep balsam, & shocked pink-&
-chartreuse suddenly flickered the shades, what's
this? Some florid spring orchard? — No,
snowblind; swept on through, shied off the wet
wads the loaded limbs sloughed only
to whip back up & knock down more, & there's

that collie snuffling the pocks, hysterical— spooked
me into the open. Lapsed snow
dangled as usual off the pine ledge halfway home &
whistled idly still, dead-to-the-world bears in its pockets.

INTERVENTION

By chance get a good look at them, three loose
backroad hounds & reacquainting: sniff,
wag, back off, hackles & dodge.
It's a time of year. Farther on, in logging slash,
the deer— by March as skinny as they get—
catch on to a situation
pretty quick & hoist themselves, each its own
one valise of the world's vitals.
Stir up in the drab days,
I'm tired of it too—
all winter, & now this.

You know the stars behind dawn
just barely shuffled, & soon
shift to shuffle out luck's tricks again—
it's his frisson uniquely, though, when the one
buck-it-is, singled out, knows he is,
& there he goes in his hock-
deep lurch in wideopen half across the lake
where his jolly pursuers skim the crust & gain—
so you pull the car over, knock at a house
they should call the warden, then maybe you watch
for if anybody saves the day.

Or, civic-duty done, drive on— you're on company time.
Might ring later from home,
backcountry personnel won't mind. Dispatch
calls who went & he calls back: dogs got that buck
down, those dogs took off at our shots & the buck
did too— maybe infected to death yet— & we tracked
those dogs clear up by Bunker Hill
& chewed out the lowlifes there to keep them tied, *vindicators*

by blue heaven & practical manners, we follow
Cro-Magnon, who coaxed a couple of wolf whelps
around the settlement garbage & founded the kingdom
of safe & sound.

PROTESTANT ARGUMENTATIVE

Jehovah's Witnesses teach that Paradise is
ordinary life here on earth, made perfect.

1.

Query me, query me
one bird adds, presumably
to another. Maybe I'm about
to wake up dead? Since when?
How would I know? Hello?

Early morning prides itself; best I get
of the time I get. Woodpecker, you may rap
yet a brisker riff & improvise on that.
On account of happiness

I babble before breakfast & circumambulate
the blooming woods, a few promiscuous refutations-on-nonsense
gleefully bounding ahead of each intuition I venture
under the sun. Ere mosquitoes
start, & deerflies
(noonish), I'll have sifted the mist's
glister to nothing-left-of-it in a hot day's
heightening blue blaze. I'll have clarified to verse.

2.

Southern Baptist step-relations
recommend death to me kindly. They aspire me off
to Heaven, a well-intentioned
(though fluffy) facility adrift above
& beyond this world. But I always do resist a trip:
transports & iffy exotic
destinations unnerve me. I like my dear
defensible nearabouts, home, right here.

I dig in. *I don't want to go.*

And if, as the Baptists hushing
my quibbles insist, our beloveds who've dearly-
defected to glory can hardly wait to celebrate
me likewise up, *I refuse.*
I cherish & choose instead these preening
hemlocks here-&-now, or, near-&-soon,

even the poorest rib-wringing rot-
hearted top-heavy balsam that creaks aloud & falls.
So there.

3.

Nag me again, Jehovah's Witnesses!
Preach me the counter-paradise
that erupts & arouses every earthly,
local, domestic, intimate thing I trust
to its daily rounds again, to thrive

innovated; itself, none other, & zapped
sublime from its core to its aura:
self-evident flesh articulate
at last of the moment's
thought God gave it. Scratch

the dirt & heave the grave! What sinister
ruse to resist if eternity strikes us hearth-
&-homely to boost the prospect a notch
from pretty-good-enough (for me),
to perfectly perfect for all?
                              High pitch
of the insects' whine zeroing in won't madden me then,
nor the sting, nor the red itch. Delighted, I'll tingle
to nourish my fellow-intricate
creatures on portions of body & blood —my own—
I'll administer then to be eaten & drunk,

as the skeeter guarantees,

praising at my temple even now.

4.

Don't bereave me,
good neighborly saints & prophets, don't leave
me to dribble my own pot of tea
& garble disputations against myself.

Pay attention! Listen to me!
Outsmart, I beg, my week's
finest rebuttals, & overwhelm
once & for all my intransigence
& grief. I will snuggle in bliss
deep into my deathbed if I can wake
adept in your most excellent chapter & verse.

Champion me, on that morning! —nudge my superb
elbow & guide me, wondering, out
from the sound porch step to the luminous pasture fence.

Motion me, "Here!" & holy blinking
cow in every prayed-for weather at once it is:
I've died & Heaven's come—

—Now you can go home.

CAROLINA

Nonentity's birthplace: a front yard sweeps
its dirt clean. Devil hopped up the oak tree,
devil-take-the-profit seized
a jay in the twigs by the feet, wings buffeting

this child's cheeks to rhyme. Leaf of gift
box tissue folded over her pocket comb. Hind
pocket kazoo. Won't somebody please start
something other & oddball soon,

narrow her down out of folly
& trivia to destiny? But Whynot the tortie cat
flopped an irregular sunny patch,
wriggles & rolls & revives the blissy fits of ignorance.

Decades crunch as minor upcountry thunder. My nod
to Mastermind's robot rabbit, said to dwell in his top
hat, who tips me a silk evening. Gloaming again & never
far from home. Listen you hoots: alas for me, for my love

with the gallant and grifter soul has tucked
into just the crevice he feared. Fear told
& tells him the truth, so he trusts it. Listen
you hollers, whatever you had in mind for me.

DOGTOOTH

Little, I learned oops-y-daisy picks up
to count off: *does love me, does not?*
Later, ontology fretted at what or
whether anything is, or isn't. The end

of the daisy's petals' detachment—
drop dead lightly— spread wings overnight
& this morning chirps elder me
errand to errand, shadow to sunspots,

as crosswalkers bow & *do allow me!*
to step street after street on ever-
strange & stranger arms, soon-to-be
offhanded, next dispelled. I miss

your distant voice in my body's
brush valleys. Your shout
vibrated the implements left behind in the haying fields,
struck the barbed wires—

No daytime since but plucks at itself, tight
bloodsucking ticks & tocks.
Night sweats: *didn't we overhear fear
most what you fear*

not at all —shambles of old shoes, tiddly
winking linoleum physiognomies,
teacup, front porch, the wicker there & the one
fist with three violets?

OVER AGAIN

Breakers stumble into & slump off
the bubbly sand, reminding
an old man he's got no use for a morning
after a yesterday morning: more

& more he's his dreams, except near
an edge of his nap sixteen gulls regroup
& gibe as water repeatedly
knocks other water down from behind.

He gets baffled about dying.
Groceries he'll need by day-
or next day-after-tomorrow—
when daughters call up, when they tell

him over again the things he already
hears from ahead of time, *Yo!*—
above a sour radio jingle, the volleyball
hollers, loose kids' dares & doubledares.

PROVISIONS

Sometimes a woman will stop to start,
she thinks, for groceries, and as if it mattered.
Bless her going out
& her coming in late next hour flourishing
celery exfoliate from two bulky bags; she
has imagined her way death-
defiantly home again from the fluorescent
acreage of goods in stock where, in a puff
of fine ash, there appeared to her

this firework: a lizard
involving the red rose— zeal, she understands.
Wrestling the petals. Flashforward
to variables of time & weather, but,
among the possible combinations, a stringy
light seems to pluck into human limbs and surroundings:
harp, with marionettes. The jitters.
She rests her head then gently in her hair.
Poise, to steer her among the aisles.

Even if the house plague
is contagion itself. Even as the peach bruise elaborates.
Seizure of the shoelace knot! At fingertips
jig the dancing dust around the dancing void, until I love
my body and soul so fervently that both
rally on the spot to what must sound exactly like my call—
out of the vast neighborhood
distances in a twinkling, sloppy with joy, each
scrambling over the other to greet me.

AFTER SUMMER

Thanks for your flesh:
I ran robberies on appletrees &
daring daylight river raids
for years for less;

hardly ever did leafiest
sunshine tip my eye to sweets as
nippy as even the kiss that once
just missed my heart,

nor ever did water alight
my lip in such silk licks or roll
my hips in so thorough a splash,
though it spilled me

under afresh & just this noon. I bewilder
myself in happiness: gala September
to turn heartbeaten shreds high color;
cool brassy breeze noise.

You were dear,
you were glad to be
at the cutting edge of any fib I told our year,
you were bright gold.

SOIREE VIVANTE

I get all regrets
to my party! So decomposes my up-to-the-last-
minute gaudy hour: yellow balloons
flaccid, the bubbly
corked in its rack. Costumed sommelier
hovering the epergne
(figment himself, & soon dismissed)
rescinds the all-but-imminent cascade.
Somebody has been saying about
me that I don't exist, I bet, & bewitching the centerpiece
petals to hurl themselves up into this brown fugue.

As if I wouldn't recognize a soul! If a soul
dropped into my party I'd nimbly
enough avert & dissemble, confide
I snuck in myself but moments ago to linger
likewise this very foyer, where no
hostess at all
bestirs a fragrance or lifts the lid
of a shadowed but brightening eye our way.
Surely some brillianter calendar
has jotted in over her instantly
null & palimpsest occasion just us two.

Just so
is all not lost. What a leggy old
geranium you lived to be, darling! the more
succulent than I'd guessed,
bowing, now, lips to my livid wrist,
first strains of a tune-to-be-soon
sidling our waists, twitching the circlet of fringe on my hips.

WHAT TIME IT GETS TO BE

I was just getting to that.
But first, old age.
If you could just let me finish.

Once it was I who rudely
interrupted proceedings: the chair rapped
& called to order, but I seized from pending

approval the minutes & ran
off with the handsome mustachioed
night watch. Matching wits we wound up
jangling on a motel
bureau in simultaneous
alarm & ran down
together to silence,

Bide-a-Wee's appointed
guest in his sleep deceased
so far from home he didn't know
a soul. A what? We heard
Gideons rustling in the drawer,

& as we rifled the fellow's bags before we fled,
& fled, his time flew too,
from his cuffs & collars flapping ahead.

EVERYBODY WAITING

Outside the flabby snow's begun to stick.
We were sure it wouldn't.
We were sure you'd've come for us by now, and
we'd all be on the
road, long gone.

You can see a couple of birds hitch up in the wind.
Nobody says much.
We could unwrap the
lunches and break some of the oranges up,
but nobody'd stop at that, we'd eat everything.

This happens and we never use the time,
because what if you turn up?
Really though some completely different
day has moved in, and we
probably aren't even in it.

ABERRATION

Fellow she picked up downtown & flirted home suddenly
veers off dead on her hip, & without
warning, o chick little, the sky starts
falling blue-flakily past the stylish bedroom's one
unoccupied window (cats
were chattering at birds in the bush at the other).
Something inconvenient has got
to be done with a body now, what?

First, though: common decency just before its practical
collapse has a say. There was that jiffy (the sky
chipped) you thought you'd cherish the very
fingernails he skimmed in the silks you'd lift
off your wrists to the void, when the ceiling
in disrepair sprinkled down on the skinless
split breasts in the kitchen sink
as their juices sank under them,

everybody marinating for love. O rue
of the day, suffice. Before the dustup, when something
about to catch her eye concerning the firmament didn't,
nor his, the stranger thing happened: her trellis
shook itself into purple blossom, waking up,
& a hummingbird pair adapted to buzz the human
staggering heart. Touch of a sweet she bit from him. Not
everything deteriorates according to plan.

Dear lady, hush. Don't go spooky, incoherent.
Incidents like this & worse befall day in & out & did
long before any flap about the blue broke— yet into
toppling cumulus fluke upon freak abandon kit
& career, municipal offices run like lunatic fringe
candidates for her life. As if less drastic
measures hadn't eluded already! —terrestrial rubble
didn't blurt up & redouble, slurry off on molten cobalt.

IMPULSE TO DISSOLUTION

Disorderly the air
tumbles, drops & plucks up dust
off the crowded grasses,
bristling legs of bees—

Unwise
of any mind of mine to let itself
get scattered so, off merrily & every
which way,

instance of busy
cellular disturbance, kind
world so agreeably
disguised—

    to catch onto that
patch of a redwing
blackbird & tatter in goldenrod.

ACCIDENTAL

Briefly come to, badly hurt,
you can guess how it is: your death
croons oo to you motherly
morning before you can flail one numb
muddy fist or kick,

& even though the ochre gully's
stout trees hold like help
& the creek bank holds its
locked rocks to locked
rocks like help, your own

other hand lets go what good
grip you had of the ground;
blood you need drains
down the clogged weeds & clears
itself through a blue

watery gravel until it rinses to such
purity that no
innuendo of body remains.
You may extricate now
from thankless tasks— but the one

you took upon yourself
in a mishap of mind, in ground fog
(when, apparently, a long shade
backed off & fingered your wet
lip, *hush*): that one presses on.

SPUTTER

Have it your own way, Paul! Let's all
relay around your hospice for weeks,
telephone, come, go, not
doing deathwatch, Paul
doesn't do death;

stuffing ourselves, talk, fill, dump the ashtrays,
rummage after something-or-other for one of the kids,
stumbling into each other, into odd chores, fits & starts.
You preside from time to time, propped up.

No doubt you intrigue it all for yourself: who
shows up when, with whom, who never does, everyone's
everlasting intricate scandals & bickerings even exiled
firmly out to the backyard more
than once, *if that's what you're gonna do,*

commotions & machinations that smart women
keep up best, whose men
nudge into it awkwardly, at cross-purposes,
& soon withdraw, hulk at each other morosely,
& head on out for the next grocery & beer run.

Overhearing, must be,
but less & less the detail of it, Paul nods, wakes, sleeps.
feels the good vibrant web hum.

***

Beach picnic, years ago.

Put Paul in his boat,
the outboard he tinkered on all winter long
so that now it didn't run differently than it didn't
run last fall:

Paul's occasion to clown his dismay for us,

fresh mechanical ingenuities, fresh dismay;
funny man, fat man, give that
sucker another finger, self-slap upside-the-head, pantomime
magic trickery, do tantrum, abject prayer, thrust in
the lewd strokes, kiss the thing like dice & yank as bright

water lapped
him gently away.

O backfires, detonations! wasn't he positive
he could tease any old ghastly motor,
get it to choke on itself & turn
itself over just one more time!

Where's the paddle now? Paul lost it out
in the middle of that enormous lake, didn't
he fuss & fume!

It got late.
He can't get home.

THE WORST OVER

Maybe sun shine, maybe
snow storm down all day,
maybe wind to hurry you or
rain, I will hurry too;

did you see the early
morning moon, can you hear the rocky
water running near to human
speech like a true story?

I looked for you all day,
I listened all night for you;
I listened all day for you and I
looked for you all night:

why are you shy, why
are you stone, why
do you dream cold colder
stone to start, stone to the end?

Anybody must keep up love enough,
anybody must work to live;
work the light in and out of the sky,
work voices into the rooms again and again:

maybe by noon, by night,
maybe by morning out at the end of
our reach you'll touch back, ask what
day is it. Is the worst over.

SPECULATION

First, from the snap's coldest wrinkly
edges the lake skins over.
Ice puts out prongs and branches
in zigzags lacing up watertight.

The skater, remembering how,
and his marvelous blades ride
like thoughts the ringing surface,
by airy scoots & curlicues, on

to the world's outermost membrane.
There he can circle inside
the seamless skies of his cells;
on their sheer mirroring floors flourish

at will & recklessly. Whether they and he
break through or not is whether the water will.

LET'S

O baby let your heart race mine
like a mill, like the rat, like the human, like the 3-
legged & sack at the company not-
going-out-of-business-after-
all bailout barbecue, kiss-&-tell the shit from the shine-
ola, ole, I love a parade.

Let's put up with each other always. Let's
make much too much of the least little thing,
kiss it & make it squeal itself well
well well. Let's wallow adversity,
pamper each other fat & contrariwise
tot up one hilarious scandal & scorn.

Death kicks every habit & bites. It's a brat.
You could say that! Christen the jetski Heavens-
to-Betsy & roar the here-be-
monsters deep to Mandalay & Crete,
to the skirling edge of the castle of teeth:
into death's whistle fling a red rose wreath.

NOTES

6 — (holy) grail— in medieval legend, the cup from which Jesus drank at the last supper. It was brought to England and lost there.

17 — Though "isolated incidents" of adulterated Halloween candy have been reported from time to time since the 1970's, SNOPES considers "random" trick-or-treat poisonings an "urban legend." Since targeting—however motivated—isn't "random," that terminology necessarily excludes racist cases from consideration.

20— "if thine eye"— New Testament, Mark 9:47

— "fierce tears"— Dylan Thomas, Do not go gentle into that good night, line 17

— "out damned Spot"— variation from Shakespeare, Macbeth, Act 5, scene 1, line 35

21— Mosaic tablets— Old Testament, Exodus 24:12 and 31:18

Hector the pup— search online. Interesting, too long for a note.

24— sepia— a reddish-brown color associated with monochrome photographs of the early 20th century

33— a grace at mealtime: "Bless this food to our use and our hands to thy service"

34— zazen— a zen Buddhist meditation, usually performed in lotus position

42— during Operation Cast Lead (2008-9), news online reported Israeli pilots boasting of their precision fire ripping up the ground of a Gaza cemetery so as to unearth and irretrievably pulverize the dead, thereby nullifying Islamic burial requirements.

44-52— Marjory Stoneman Douglas' *River of Grass*, which I thought would be about animal, vegetable, and earth-science phenomena, proved (to me) surprisingly political.

46— The US built the Nike-Hercules missile site in Everglades National Park in 1964, to address Cuba. Now deactivated, the installation is available to tours.

49— Flandrian Transgression, a term of geomorphology, refers to the global warming and glacial melt during the Holocene, when the rising ocean water changed the shape of Florida above sea level.

51— Continental drift split the original Pangaea landmass, separating the Americas from Africa such that what is now Florida departed from what is now Senegal.

52— pneumatophores— the aerial roots of mangrove, specialized for gas exchange, poke up vertically out of the ground all around the base of the tree.

— vegetable Moseses— Old Testament, Exodus 2:1-6. Mangrove sprouts float the shallows until they develop one weighted end that tips them vertical. As the heavy end sinks lower, touching bottom stimulates the cells to produce an anchoring root.

57—grandmother's trunk— a child's alphabet game

— ankus— an elephant goad, consisting of a spear tip and a hook.

— howdah— a seat, sometimes canopied, for riding on an elephant's back

63— by their fruits— New Testament, Matthew 7:16 and 7:20

67— sparrow— New Testament, Matthew 10:29, ff.

69— nothing from nothing— an old maxim. Parmenides, Shakespeare (King Lear, Act 1, scene 1, line 92) and many other sources.

72— remuda— a herd of saddle-broken horses to choose a mount from

80— going out and coming in— Old Testament, Deuteronomy 28:4-6, depending on the translation. Often adapted into prayers and meditations.

82— Soiree Vivante— my variation on tableau vivant, a scene, usually from a painting, represented by living people.

85— chick little— folk tale character. Alarmist Chicken Little disrupted barnyard tranquillity by running around hollering that the sky was falling.

92— here be monsters— inscription by cartographers on old nautical maps, to indicate uncharted regions.

ACKNOWLEDGMENTS

99 Poems for the 99% (online): White Phosphorus (reprint)
ABZ: Pachyderm
Alaska Quarterly Review: Preacherbird
The American Voice: Custodial
Boston Review: Let's; Overturn
Cerise Press (online): Aberration; Pledge; Soiree Vivante; Spite Face
The Chattahoochee Review: Professional Sleep; Real Estate
The Chicago Review: Towns
Conduit: Erotic Complaint
Crazyhorse: Abracadabra; Ophthalmology
Denver Quarterly: Ding; Everglades Field Journal
Epoch: Foxfire; Fictor's Triolet; Over Again
Field: To Distraction; Wattle & Daub
Generation: Impulse to Dissolution; Irrelevance of Angels
The Gettysburg Review: Contretemps; Pinch Me
Green Mountains Review: Alligator Resolve; Railroad Moon, Welcome to Senegal
Hampden-Sydney Poetry Review: Dogtooth; Intervention; Pendulum
Indiana Review: Night Owl
The Journal: Anhinga Trail, With Seminole Wars
Manoa: Everybody Waiting; Sepia (as Spring Thaw); What Becomes of Them
The Marlboro Review: Mangrove Bride
The National Poetry Review: Mr. Bluster Housesits; Rebirthday
New Letters: Still Hungry
New Orleans Review: Accidental; Astral & Mundane; The Bats; Domestic; Rat Song With Undertones
New Voices: Speculation
The New York Quarterly: Stone Song
The North American Review: White Phosphorus
Northwest Review: Calling; March Archaic
The Paris Review: Shingle
Pequod: Advice
Perihelion: Cross-Country; Outfit; Portrait
Poetry: Carolina; What Time It Gets to Be; Whereabouts
Poetry Daily (online) Overturn (reprint)
Poetry Northwest: Sputter; Landslide
Prairie Schooner: Pomegranate

Room of One's Own: Nuptial; Terms
San Fernando Poetry Journal: Stan Frees the Cats
Smartish Pace: Cows; Protestant Argumentative
Southern Poetry Review: By Way of Illustration; Ebb; Flandrian Transgression
Sou'wester: At Leisure (as Occasional); Exploratory (as They Never Tell You)
Verse Daily (online): Ebb (reprint, & named a *Verse Daily* favorite)
The Virginia Quarterly Review: Provisions
Yellow Silk: After Summer

The Vermont Arts Council published the author's chapbook, *Powers*, which collected "Everybody Waiting," an earlier version of "Orange Persona with Trigger Warnings" then titled "Last Week to Lay Bets on the Election," "Procedure" (as "Abortion"), " "Sepia" (as "Spring Thaw"), "She Listens," "Exploratory" (as "They Never Tell You"), "Towns," and "The Worst Over."

I thank the University of Michigan, for Avery Hopwood and Jule Hopwood Awards for a manuscript including "Irrelevance of Angels;" The Vermont Studio Center; Agha Shahid Ali; Reginald Gibbons; Tom Lux; Heather McHugh, Steve Orlen and the Warren Wilson College Master of Fine Arts Program for Writers, also Pat and Burt Corbus, Muriel Nelson, Dawnine Spivak, Samn Stockwell, and Ann Turkle. Poems comprising the section A STRANGE PLACE were largely composed during an Everglades National Park Artist in Residency Program; thanks again to Donna Marxer and Anne McCrary Sullivan.

www.ingramcontent.com/pod-product-compliance
Lightning Source LLC
Chambersburg PA
CBHW050502110426
42742CB00018B/3346